This journal belongs to

_____

_____

_____

MANIFESTATION

JOURNAL

HOW TO USE THIS JOURNAL

This journal is designed to help you on your manifesting journey by providing 90 days of writing prompts that serve as a guide to maintain your vibrational energy while manifesting. Below are some tips on how to use the prompts provided so you get the most out of this journal and your manifesting experience.

My Manifestation

Get Clear On What You Want To Manifest

Write down what you want to manifest. Be as specific as possible when it comes to articulating your wish. So instead of writing "I want to have a successful career," write something like "I want to earn six-figures coaching five clients by the end of this year".

Uncover Your Why

Once you have determined what you want, write down why you want these things. This way, you can ensure you truly want what you think you want - and for the right reasons. Ask yourself questions like: What brings me true joy?, What lights me up? or What would my ideal day look like?

When you know what you want and why, you know where you are headed and you are not so easily distracted. You can respond to the challenges and opportunities that come your way, because you are not troubled by conflicting feelings and unconscious motivations.

Letter To The Universe

Now that you have clearly identified what you want and why, it is time to ask the universe for it. Write a letter to the universe to put your request out there. There is no right or wrong way of doing this just let your thoughts flow freely.

My Future Looks Like

Sit in a comfortable position, close your eyes and imagine – in as vivid detail as you can – what your dream life looks like. The more real it seems, the easier you will find it to both believe it will happen and gain the motivation to work towards achieving it.

Visualising in this way will activate your subconscious which will start generating creative ideas to achieve your goals.

It also activates the law of attraction, drawing into your life the people, resources, and circumstances you will need to achieve your goals.

Removing Blocks

One of the most common challenges that can interfere with manifestation are a negative mindset, self-doubt and limiting beliefs.

By being vigilant and aware of forces that are energetically holding you back from manifesting your dreams you can address them, and move past them.

Use the page "Removing Blocks" to help you transform limiting beliefs into positive thoughts and affirmations.

You can come back to this page any time during the 3 months of journaling when you feel negative thoughts overtake.

Weekly Scripting Page

Set A Weekly Intention

An intention is a powerful, positive and purposeful phrase that helps guide your choices as you go through your week.

How To Choose

What are the two to three most important things you want to accomplish in your life?

Is there a role in your life you feel compelled to succeed at?

What current healthy life change are you pursuing?

When you close your eyes at night, what daily pursuit or accomplishment leaves you feeling the most fulfilled?

The Difference Between Goals And Intentions

Goals are focused on the future. They are about a destination or a specific achievement.

Intentions are in the present moment. They are lived each day, independent of reaching the goal or destination. They are about the inner relationship with yourself. Intentions give you the daily rhythm, motivation and accountability you need to transform yourself.

By being intentional you will enjoy the journey as much as the destination, and therefore bring more joy to everything you are doing.

A weekly intention could sound like this: This week, I will bring balance and space into my schedule to create time for the people and passions that matter most to my soul. Refresh your intention during the week.

Pick Your Top 3 Priorities For The Week

You can't do it all and you shouldn't try. You can actually have a more productive week by eliminating things off your to-do list and prioritise the few things that are most important.

Endless to-do lists are daunting. It can be helpful to create a master to-do list of everything that needs done, but don't work from your master to-do list.

Instead, pick your top 3 priorities for the week. If you could only get 3 things done, what would they be? Write them down and then break each priority down into smaller tasks until you have completed them.

Once you have completed all 3 priorities you are free to move on to your next 3 most important tasks.

Weekly Goal And Intentional Action Steps

Pick one goal for the week. Starting with one of your goals allows you to narrow your focus enough to achieve it. It is better to start with one goal and complete it than to start with three and not complete any.

Create a list of intentional action steps you need to take to achieve your goal. It is not enough to just wait for them to come true. By taking even the smallest action toward your dreams, you will increase your odds of manifesting them.

Daily Scripting Pages

The daily scripting pages will help to bring your awareness and intention to the day. This way you are more likely to make conscious choices in actions and attitudes as the day unfolds.

Pay Attention To Your Feelings

Here you can note down how you want to feel today. This is an important aspect of manifesting that is often overlooked. Many people approach manifestation from a place of "How can I get something to feel better?" Instead, the focus should be: "How can I feel better and therefore be an energetic match for attracting more greatness into my life?"

Make sure to stay committed to the goal of feeling good first and attracting things second. After all, when your primary function is to be happy, then whatever comes to you is irrelevant. Happiness is your true manifestation.

Express gratitude

Developing an attitude of gratitude results in more positive life outcomes, greater sense of happiness and a higher degree of satisfaction. Fill the daily gratitude list with things or people you are grateful for. This will lift your mood and get you into the state of thinking and feeling more positive.

Manifestation Affirmations

Affirmations are positive statements designed to eliminate negative self-talk and to reinforce empowering thoughts about your ability to achieve your dreams.

Start your affirmations with "I am..." like "I am full of life and filled with possibility" or "I am on the right path. I am moving in the right direction" or "I am not the negative thoughts I think". You will find affirmations at the end of this book to use in your daily journaling.

And finally, even though it may feel hard at times to put your faith in something you can not see or know with certainty, it is critical to believe in order to receive from the universe.

You may have heard of the "Law of Attraction" and that is exactly what is at play when you are manifesting. The Law of Attraction refers to our ability to attract what we believe. So, if you believe good things will happen, you will attract good things. On the contrary, if you don't believe good things will happen they won't.

Let go of how and when and trust that you will get what you want when the time is right.

● ● ● ● ● ●

WHAT YOU THINK,

YOU BECOME.

WHAT YOU FEEL,

YOU ATTRACT.

WHAT YOU IMAGINE,

YOU CREATE.

BUDDHA

My Manifestation

I WANT TO MANIFEST ...

WHY DO I WANT TO MANIFEST THIS?

HOW AM I GOING TO FEEL?

WHAT WILL MY LIFE LOOK LIKE?

LETTER TO THE UNIVERSE

DATE: ....

LETTER TO THE UNIVERSE

DATE:

MY FUTURE LOOKS LIKE ...

DATE: ....

MY FUTURE LOOKS LIKE ...

DATE:

REMOVING BLOCKS

LIMITING BELIEF   ➙   NEW BELIEF

LIMITING BELIEF   ➙   NEW BELIEF

LIMITING BELIEF   ➙   NEW BELIEF

LIMITING BELIEF   ➙   NEW BELIEF

LIMITING BELIEF   ➙   NEW BELIEF

LIMITING BELIEF   ➙   NEW BELIEF

WEEK OF

J F M A M J
J A S O N D

INTENTION FOR THE WEEK

TOP 3 PRIORITIES

#**1**

#**2**

#**3**

THIS WEEK'S GOAL

INTENTIONAL ACTION STEPS

○
○
○
○
○
○
○
○
○

TRACKER	MO	TU	WE	TH	FR	SA	SU
Daily Gratitude	○	○	○	○	○	○	○
Affirmations	○	○	○	○	○	○	○
Visualization	○	○	○	○	○	○	○
Meditation	○	○	○	○	○	○	○
	○	○	○	○	○	○	○
	○	○	○	○	○	○	○
	○	○	○	○	○	○	○
	○	○	○	○	○	○	○

Monday

I AM MANIFESTING ...

....
....
....
....

HOW DO I WANT TO FEEL TODAY?

....
....
....

TODAY I AM GRATEFUL FOR ...

♡ _____

♡ _____

♡ _____

♡ _____

♡ _____

♡ _____

♡ _____

♡ _____

♡ _____

INTENTION FOR THE DAY

MY DAILY AFFIRMATIONS

● ....

● ....

● ....

● ....

● ....

Tuesday

I AM MANIFESTING ...

....

....

....

....

HOW DO I WANT TO FEEL TODAY?

....

....

....

....

INTENTION FOR THE DAY

TODAY I AM GRATEFUL FOR ...

♡ ....

♡ ....

♡ ....

♡ ....

♡ ....

♡ ....

♡ ....

♡ ....

♡ ....

MY DAILY AFFIRMATIONS

● ....

● ....

● ....

● ....

● ....

Wednesday

I AM MANIFESTING ...

....

....

....

....

HOW DO I WANT TO FEEL TODAY?

TODAY I AM GRATEFUL FOR ...

♡

♡

♡

♡

♡

♡

♡

♡

♡

INTENTION FOR THE DAY

MY DAILY AFFIRMATIONS

-
-
-
-
-

Thursday

DATE: _____

I AM MANIFESTING ...

....

....

....

....

HOW DO I WANT TO FEEL TODAY?

....

....

....

TODAY I AM GRATEFUL FOR ...

♡ ....

♡ ....

♡ ....

♡ ....

♡ ....

♡ ....

♡ ....

♡ ....

♡ ....

INTENTION FOR THE DAY

MY DAILY AFFIRMATIONS

● ....

● ....

● ....

● ....

● ....

Friday

I AM MANIFESTING ...

HOW DO I WANT TO FEEL TODAY?

TODAY I AM GRATEFUL FOR ...

♡

♡

♡

♡

♡

♡

♡

♡

♡

INTENTION FOR THE DAY

MY DAILY AFFIRMATIONS

-
-
-
-
-

Saturday

DATE: ....

I AM MANIFESTING ...

....

....

....

....

HOW DO I WANT TO FEEL TODAY?

....

....

....

INTENTION FOR THE DAY

TODAY I AM GRATEFUL FOR ...

♡

♡

♡

♡

♡

♡

♡

♡

♡

MY DAILY AFFIRMATIONS

● ....

● ....

● ....

● ....

● ....

Sunday

I AM MANIFESTING ...

HOW DO I WANT TO FEEL TODAY?

TODAY I AM GRATEFUL FOR ...

♡

♡

♡

♡

♡

♡

♡

♡

♡

INTENTION FOR THE DAY

MY DAILY AFFIRMATIONS

- ●
- ●
- ●
- ●
- ●

WEEK OF

(J) (F) (M) (A) (M) (J)
(J) (A) (S) (O) (N) (D)

INTENTION FOR THE WEEK

TOP 3 PRIORITIES

#1 ....

#2 ....

#3 ....

THIS WEEK'S GOAL

INTENTIONAL ACTION STEPS

○
○
○
○
○
○
○
○
○

TRACKER	MO	TU	WE	TH	FR	SA	SU
Daily Gratitude	○	○	○	○	○	○	○
Affirmations	○	○	○	○	○	○	○
Visualization	○	○	○	○	○	○	○
Meditation	○	○	○	○	○	○	○
	○	○	○	○	○	○	○
	○	○	○	○	○	○	○
	○	○	○	○	○	○	○
	○	○	○	○	○	○	○

Monday

DATE: ....

I AM MANIFESTING ...

....
....
....
....

HOW DO I WANT TO FEEL TODAY?

....
....
....

INTENTION FOR THE DAY

TODAY I AM GRATEFUL FOR ...

♡ ....
♡ ....
♡ ....
♡ ....
♡ ....
♡ ....
♡ ....
♡ ....
♡ ....

MY DAILY AFFIRMATIONS

● ....
● ....
● ....
● ....
● ....

Tuesday

I AM MANIFESTING ...

....
....
....
....

HOW DO I WANT TO FEEL TODAY?

....

....

....

INTENTION FOR THE DAY

TODAY I AM GRATEFUL FOR ...

♡ ....

♡ ....

♡ ....

♡ ....

♡ ....

♡ ....

♡ ....

♡ ....

♡ ....

MY DAILY AFFIRMATIONS

● ....

● ....

● ....

● ....

● ....

Wednesday

DATE:

I AM MANIFESTING ...

HOW DO I WANT TO FEEL TODAY?

TODAY I AM GRATEFUL FOR ...

♡

♡

♡

♡

♡

♡

♡

♡

♡

INTENTION FOR THE DAY

MY DAILY AFFIRMATIONS

-
-
-
-
-

Thursday

DATE:

I AM MANIFESTING ...

HOW DO I WANT TO FEEL TODAY?

TODAY I AM GRATEFUL FOR ...

♡

♡

♡

♡

♡

♡

♡

♡

♡

INTENTION FOR THE DAY

MY DAILY AFFIRMATIONS

-
-
-
-
-

Friday

DATE: ....

I AM MANIFESTING ...

....
....
....
....

HOW DO I WANT TO FEEL TODAY?

....
....
....

TODAY I AM GRATEFUL FOR ...

♡
♡
♡
♡
♡
♡
♡
♡
♡

INTENTION FOR THE DAY

MY DAILY AFFIRMATIONS

-
-
-
-
-

Saturday

DATE: ....

I AM MANIFESTING ...

....
....
....
....

HOW DO I WANT TO FEEL TODAY?

....
....
....

TODAY I AM GRATEFUL FOR ...

♡ ....
♡ ....
♡ ....
♡ ....
♡ ....
♡ ....
♡ ....
♡ ....
♡ ....

INTENTION FOR THE DAY

MY DAILY AFFIRMATIONS

● ....
● ....
● ....
● ....
● ....

Sunday

DATE: ....

I AM MANIFESTING ...

....
....
....
....

HOW DO I WANT TO FEEL TODAY?

....
....
....

INTENTION FOR THE DAY

TODAY I AM GRATEFUL FOR ...

♡ ....
♡ ....
♡ ....
♡ ....
♡ ....
♡ ....
♡ ....
♡ ....
♡ ....

MY DAILY AFFIRMATIONS

● ....
● ....
● ....
● ....
● ....

WEEK OF

(J) (F) (M) (A) (M) (J)
(J) (A) (S) (O) (N) (D)

INTENTION FOR THE WEEK

TOP 3 PRIORITIES

#1 ....

#2 ....

#3 ....

THIS WEEK'S GOAL

INTENTIONAL ACTION STEPS

◯

◯

◯

◯

◯

◯

◯

◯

◯

TRACKER	MO	TU	WE	TH	FR	SA	SU
Daily Gratitude	◯	◯	◯	◯	◯	◯	◯
Affirmations	◯	◯	◯	◯	◯	◯	◯
Visualization	◯	◯	◯	◯	◯	◯	◯
Meditation	◯	◯	◯	◯	◯	◯	◯
	◯	◯	◯	◯	◯	◯	◯
	◯	◯	◯	◯	◯	◯	◯
	◯	◯	◯	◯	◯	◯	◯
	◯	◯	◯	◯	◯	◯	◯

Monday

I AM MANIFESTING ...

....

....

....

HOW DO I WANT TO FEEL TODAY?

....

....

....

TODAY I AM GRATEFUL FOR ...

♡ ....

♡ ....

♡ ....

♡ ....

♡ ....

♡ ....

♡ ....

♡ ....

♡ ....

INTENTION FOR THE DAY

MY DAILY AFFIRMATIONS

● ....

● ....

● ....

● ....

● ....

Tuesday

DATE: _____

I AM MANIFESTING ...

....

....

....

HOW DO I WANT TO FEEL TODAY?

....

....

....

INTENTION FOR THE DAY

TODAY I AM GRATEFUL FOR ...

♡ ....

♡ ....

♡ ....

♡ ....

♡ ....

♡ ....

♡ ....

♡ ....

MY DAILY AFFIRMATIONS

● ....

● ....

● ....

● ....

● ....

Wednesday

I AM MANIFESTING ...

HOW DO I WANT TO FEEL TODAY?

TODAY I AM GRATEFUL FOR ...

♡

♡

♡

♡

♡

♡

♡

♡

♡

INTENTION FOR THE DAY

MY DAILY AFFIRMATIONS

●

●

●

●

●

Thursday

I AM MANIFESTING ...

HOW DO I WANT TO FEEL TODAY?

TODAY I AM GRATEFUL FOR ...

♡

♡

♡

♡

♡

♡

♡

♡

♡

INTENTION FOR THE DAY

MY DAILY AFFIRMATIONS

●

●

●

●

●

Friday

I AM MANIFESTING ...

....

....

....

....

HOW DO I WANT TO FEEL TODAY?

....

....

....

TODAY I AM GRATEFUL FOR ...

♡ ....

♡ ....

♡ ....

♡ ....

♡ ....

♡ ....

♡ ....

♡ ....

♡ ....

INTENTION FOR THE DAY

MY DAILY AFFIRMATIONS

● ....

● ....

● ....

● ....

● ....

Saturday

DATE:

I AM MANIFESTING ...

HOW DO I WANT TO FEEL TODAY?

TODAY I AM GRATEFUL FOR ...

♡

♡

♡

♡

♡

♡

♡

♡

♡

INTENTION FOR THE DAY

MY DAILY AFFIRMATIONS

-
-
-
-
-

Sunday

DATE:

I AM MANIFESTING ...

HOW DO I WANT TO FEEL TODAY?

TODAY I AM GRATEFUL FOR ...

♡

♡

♡

♡

♡

♡

♡

♡

♡

INTENTION FOR THE DAY

MY DAILY AFFIRMATIONS

●

●

●

●

●

WEEK OF

J F M A M J
J A S O N D

INTENTION FOR THE WEEK

TOP 3 PRIORITIES

#1

#2

#3

THIS WEEK'S GOAL

INTENTIONAL ACTION STEPS

○
○
○
○
○
○
○
○
○

TRACKER	MO	TU	WE	TH	FR	SA	SU
Daily Gratitude	○	○	○	○	○	○	○
Affirmations	○	○	○	○	○	○	○
Visualization	○	○	○	○	○	○	○
Meditation	○	○	○	○	○	○	○
	○	○	○	○	○	○	○
	○	○	○	○	○	○	○
	○	○	○	○	○	○	○
	○	○	○	○	○	○	○

Monday

DATE: _____

I AM MANIFESTING ...

....
....
....
....

HOW DO I WANT TO FEEL TODAY?

....
....

TODAY I AM GRATEFUL FOR ...

♡ ....
♡ ....
♡ ....
♡ ....
♡ ....
♡ ....
♡ ....
♡ ....
♡ ....

INTENTION FOR THE DAY

MY DAILY AFFIRMATIONS

● ....
● ....
● ....
● ....
● ....

Tuesday

DATE: ....

I AM MANIFESTING ...

HOW DO I WANT TO FEEL TODAY?

TODAY I AM GRATEFUL FOR ...

♡

♡

♡

♡

♡

♡

♡

♡

♡

INTENTION FOR THE DAY

MY DAILY AFFIRMATIONS

-
-
-
-
-

Wednesday

DATE:

I AM MANIFESTING ...

HOW DO I WANT TO FEEL TODAY?

TODAY I AM GRATEFUL FOR ...

♡

♡

♡

♡

♡

♡

♡

♡

♡

INTENTION FOR THE DAY

MY DAILY AFFIRMATIONS

●

●

●

●

●

Thursday

DATE:

I AM MANIFESTING ...

HOW DO I WANT TO FEEL TODAY?

TODAY I AM GRATEFUL FOR ...

♡

♡

♡

♡

♡

♡

♡

♡

♡

INTENTION FOR THE DAY

MY DAILY AFFIRMATIONS

Friday

I AM MANIFESTING ...

....

....

....

....

HOW DO I WANT TO FEEL TODAY?

....

....

....

TODAY I AM GRATEFUL FOR ...

♡

♡

♡

♡

♡

♡

♡

♡

♡

INTENTION FOR THE DAY

MY DAILY AFFIRMATIONS

● ....

● ....

● ....

● ....

● ....

Saturday

DATE: _____

I AM MANIFESTING ...

_____
_____
_____
_____

HOW DO I WANT TO FEEL TODAY?

_____
_____
_____

INTENTION FOR THE DAY

TODAY I AM GRATEFUL FOR ...

♡ _____
♡ _____
♡ _____
♡ _____
♡ _____
♡ _____
♡ _____
♡ _____
♡ _____

MY DAILY AFFIRMATIONS

● _____
● _____
● _____
● _____
● _____

Sunday

DATE:

I AM MANIFESTING ...

HOW DO I WANT TO FEEL TODAY?

TODAY I AM GRATEFUL FOR ...

♡

♡

♡

♡

♡

♡

♡

♡

♡

INTENTION FOR THE DAY

MY DAILY AFFIRMATIONS

●

●

●

●

●

WEEK OF

(J) (F) (M) (A) (M) (J)
(J) (A) (S) (O) (N) (D)

INTENTION FOR THE WEEK

TOP 3 PRIORITIES

#**1**

#**2**

#**3**

THIS WEEK'S GOAL

INTENTIONAL ACTION STEPS

◯
◯
◯
◯
◯
◯
◯
◯
◯

TRACKER	MO	TU	WE	TH	FR	SA	SU
Daily Gratitude	◯	◯	◯	◯	◯	◯	◯
Affirmations	◯	◯	◯	◯	◯	◯	◯
Visualization	◯	◯	◯	◯	◯	◯	◯
Meditation	◯	◯	◯	◯	◯	◯	◯
	◯	◯	◯	◯	◯	◯	◯
	◯	◯	◯	◯	◯	◯	◯
	◯	◯	◯	◯	◯	◯	◯
	◯	◯	◯	◯	◯	◯	◯

Monday

DATE:

I AM MANIFESTING ...

HOW DO I WANT TO FEEL TODAY?

TODAY I AM GRATEFUL FOR ...

♡

♡

♡

♡

♡

♡

♡

♡

♡

INTENTION FOR THE DAY

MY DAILY AFFIRMATIONS

●

●

●

●

●

Tuesday

DATE:

I AM MANIFESTING ...

HOW DO I WANT TO FEEL TODAY?

TODAY I AM GRATEFUL FOR ...

♡

♡

♡

♡

♡

♡

♡

♡

♡

INTENTION FOR THE DAY

MY DAILY AFFIRMATIONS

-
-
-
-
-

Wednesday

I AM MANIFESTING ...

HOW DO I WANT TO FEEL TODAY?

TODAY I AM GRATEFUL FOR ...

♡

♡

♡

♡

♡

♡

♡

♡

♡

INTENTION FOR THE DAY

MY DAILY AFFIRMATIONS

-
-
-
-
-

Thursday

DATE: ....

I AM MANIFESTING ...

....

....

....

HOW DO I WANT TO FEEL TODAY?

....

....

....

TODAY I AM GRATEFUL FOR ...

♡ ....

♡ ....

♡ ....

♡ ....

♡ ....

♡ ....

♡ ....

♡ ....

♡ ....

INTENTION FOR THE DAY

MY DAILY AFFIRMATIONS

● ....

● ....

● ....

● ....

● ....

Friday

DATE:

I AM MANIFESTING ...

HOW DO I WANT TO FEEL TODAY?

TODAY I AM GRATEFUL FOR ...

♡

♡

♡

♡

♡

♡

♡

♡

♡

INTENTION FOR THE DAY

MY DAILY AFFIRMATIONS

●

●

●

●

●

Saturday

I AM MANIFESTING ...

HOW DO I WANT TO FEEL TODAY?

TODAY I AM GRATEFUL FOR ...

♡

♡

♡

♡

♡

♡

♡

♡

♡

INTENTION FOR THE DAY

MY DAILY AFFIRMATIONS

Sunday

DATE: _____

I AM MANIFESTING ...

....

....

....

HOW DO I WANT TO FEEL TODAY?

....

....

....

TODAY I AM GRATEFUL FOR ...

♡ ....

♡ ....

♡ ....

♡ ....

♡ ....

♡ ....

♡ ....

♡ ....

♡ ....

INTENTION FOR THE DAY

MY DAILY AFFIRMATIONS

● ....

● ....

● ....

● ....

● ....

WEEK OF

(J) (F) (M) (A) (M) (J)
(J) (A) (S) (O) (N) (D)

INTENTION FOR THE WEEK

TOP 3 PRIORITIES

#**1**

#**2**

#**3**

INTENTIONAL ACTION STEPS

- ◯
- ◯
- ◯
- ◯
- ◯
- ◯
- ◯
- ◯
- ◯

THIS WEEK'S GOAL

TRACKER	MO	TU	WE	TH	FR	SA	SU
Daily Gratitude	◯	◯	◯	◯	◯	◯	◯
Affirmations	◯	◯	◯	◯	◯	◯	◯
Visualization	◯	◯	◯	◯	◯	◯	◯
Meditation	◯	◯	◯	◯	◯	◯	◯
	◯	◯	◯	◯	◯	◯	◯
	◯	◯	◯	◯	◯	◯	◯
	◯	◯	◯	◯	◯	◯	◯
	◯	◯	◯	◯	◯	◯	◯

Monday

DATE:

I AM MANIFESTING ...

HOW DO I WANT TO FEEL TODAY?

TODAY I AM GRATEFUL FOR ...

♡

♡

♡

♡

♡

♡

♡

♡

♡

INTENTION FOR THE DAY

MY DAILY AFFIRMATIONS

●

●

●

●

●

Tuesday

DATE: _____

I AM MANIFESTING ...

_____

_____

_____

_____

HOW DO I WANT TO FEEL TODAY?

TODAY I AM GRATEFUL FOR ...

♡ _____

♡ _____

♡ _____

♡ _____

INTENTION FOR THE DAY

♡ _____

♡ _____

♡ _____

♡ _____

♡ _____

MY DAILY AFFIRMATIONS

● _____

● _____

● _____

● _____

● _____

Wednesday

I AM MANIFESTING ...

HOW DO I WANT TO FEEL TODAY?

TODAY I AM GRATEFUL FOR ...

♡

♡

♡

♡

♡

♡

♡

♡

♡

INTENTION FOR THE DAY

MY DAILY AFFIRMATIONS

Thursday

DATE: _____

I AM MANIFESTING ...

....

....

....

....

HOW DO I WANT TO FEEL TODAY?

....

....

....

INTENTION FOR THE DAY

TODAY I AM GRATEFUL FOR ...

♡

♡

♡

♡

♡

♡

♡

♡

♡

MY DAILY AFFIRMATIONS

● ....

● ....

● ....

● ....

● ....

Friday

DATE: ....

I AM MANIFESTING ...

....

....

....

....

HOW DO I WANT TO FEEL TODAY?

....

....

....

TODAY I AM GRATEFUL FOR ...

♡

♡

♡

♡

♡

♡

♡

♡

♡

INTENTION FOR THE DAY

MY DAILY AFFIRMATIONS

- ....
- ....
- ....
- ....
- ....

Saturday

DATE: ....

I AM MANIFESTING ...

....

....

....

....

HOW DO I WANT TO FEEL TODAY?

....

....

....

TODAY I AM GRATEFUL FOR ...

♡ ....

♡ ....

♡ ....

♡ ....

♡ ....

♡ ....

♡ ....

♡ ....

INTENTION FOR THE DAY

MY DAILY AFFIRMATIONS

● ....

● ....

● ....

● ....

● ....

Sunday

DATE:

I AM MANIFESTING ...

HOW DO I WANT TO FEEL TODAY?

TODAY I AM GRATEFUL FOR ...

♡

♡

♡

♡

♡

♡

♡

♡

♡

INTENTION FOR THE DAY

MY DAILY AFFIRMATIONS

●

●

●

●

●

WEEK OF

J F M A M J
J A S O N D

INTENTION FOR THE WEEK

TOP 3 PRIORITIES

#1

#2

#3

THIS WEEK'S GOAL

INTENTIONAL ACTION STEPS

○
○
○
○
○
○
○
○
○

TRACKER	MO	TU	WE	TH	FR	SA	SU
Daily Gratitude	○	○	○	○	○	○	○
Affirmations	○	○	○	○	○	○	○
Visualization	○	○	○	○	○	○	○
Meditation	○	○	○	○	○	○	○
	○	○	○	○	○	○	○
	○	○	○	○	○	○	○
	○	○	○	○	○	○	○
	○	○	○	○	○	○	○

Monday

DATE: _____

I AM MANIFESTING ...

....

....

....

....

....

HOW DO I WANT TO FEEL TODAY?

....

....

....

TODAY I AM GRATEFUL FOR ...

♡ ....

♡ ....

♡ ....

♡ ....

♡ ....

♡ ....

♡ ....

♡ ....

♡ ....

INTENTION FOR THE DAY

MY DAILY AFFIRMATIONS

● ....

● ....

● ....

● ....

● ....

Tuesday

DATE: _____

I AM MANIFESTING ...

_____

. . . .

. . . .

. . . .

HOW DO I WANT TO FEEL TODAY?

TODAY I AM GRATEFUL FOR ...

♡ _____

♡ _____

♡ _____

♡ _____

INTENTION FOR THE DAY

♡ _____

♡ _____

♡ _____

♡ _____

♡ _____

MY DAILY AFFIRMATIONS

- ●
- ●
- ●
- ●
- ●

Wednesday

I AM MANIFESTING ...

HOW DO I WANT TO FEEL TODAY?

TODAY I AM GRATEFUL FOR ...

♡

♡

♡

♡

INTENTION FOR THE DAY

♡

♡

♡

♡

♡

MY DAILY AFFIRMATIONS

●

●

●

●

●

Thursday

DATE: _____

I AM MANIFESTING ...

_____

....

....

....

....

HOW DO I WANT TO FEEL TODAY?

....

....

....

INTENTION FOR THE DAY

TODAY I AM GRATEFUL FOR ...

♡ _____

♡ _____

♡ _____

♡ _____

♡ _____

♡ _____

♡ _____

♡ _____

♡ _____

MY DAILY AFFIRMATIONS

● _____

● _____

● _____

● _____

● _____

Friday

I AM MANIFESTING ...

....

....

....

....

....

HOW DO I WANT TO FEEL TODAY?

....

....

....

TODAY I AM GRATEFUL FOR ...

♡ ....

♡ ....

♡ ....

♡ ....

♡ ....

♡ ....

♡ ....

♡ ....

♡ ....

INTENTION FOR THE DAY

MY DAILY AFFIRMATIONS

● ....

● ....

● ....

● ....

● ....

Saturday

DATE:

I AM MANIFESTING ...

HOW DO I WANT TO FEEL TODAY?

TODAY I AM GRATEFUL FOR ...

♡

♡

♡

♡

♡

♡

♡

♡

♡

INTENTION FOR THE DAY

MY DAILY AFFIRMATIONS

●

●

●

●

●

Sunday

DATE:

I AM MANIFESTING ...

HOW DO I WANT TO FEEL TODAY?

TODAY I AM GRATEFUL FOR ...

♡

♡

♡

♡

♡

♡

♡

♡

♡

INTENTION FOR THE DAY

MY DAILY AFFIRMATIONS

●

●

●

●

●

WEEK OF

(J) (F) (M) (A) (M) (J)
(J) (A) (S) (O) (N) (D)

INTENTION FOR THE WEEK

TOP 3 PRIORITIES

#1

#2

#3

THIS WEEK'S GOAL

INTENTIONAL ACTION STEPS

○
○
○
○
○
○
○
○
○

TRACKER	MO	TU	WE	TH	FR	SA	SU
Daily Gratitude	○	○	○	○	○	○	○
Affirmations	○	○	○	○	○	○	○
Visualization	○	○	○	○	○	○	○
Meditation	○	○	○	○	○	○	○
	○	○	○	○	○	○	○
	○	○	○	○	○	○	○
	○	○	○	○	○	○	○
	○	○	○	○	○	○	○

Monday

I AM MANIFESTING ...

....

....

....

....

HOW DO I WANT TO FEEL TODAY?

....

....

....

TODAY I AM GRATEFUL FOR ...

♡ ....

♡ ....

♡ ....

♡ ....

♡ ....

♡ ....

♡ ....

♡ ....

♡ ....

INTENTION FOR THE DAY

MY DAILY AFFIRMATIONS

● ....

● ....

● ....

● ....

● ....

Tuesday

DATE: _____

I AM MANIFESTING ...

....

....

....

....

HOW DO I WANT TO FEEL TODAY?

....

....

....

TODAY I AM GRATEFUL FOR ...

♡ ....

♡ ....

♡ ....

♡ ....

♡ ....

♡ ....

♡ ....

♡ ....

♡ ....

INTENTION FOR THE DAY

MY DAILY AFFIRMATIONS

- ....
- ....
- ....
- ....
- ....

Wednesday

I AM MANIFESTING ...

....

....

....

....

HOW DO I WANT TO FEEL TODAY?

....

....

TODAY I AM GRATEFUL FOR ...

♡ ....

♡ ....

♡ ....

♡ ....

♡ ....

♡ ....

♡ ....

♡ ....

♡ ....

INTENTION FOR THE DAY

MY DAILY AFFIRMATIONS

● ....

● ....

● ....

● ....

● ....

Thursday

DATE:

I AM MANIFESTING ...

HOW DO I WANT TO FEEL TODAY?

TODAY I AM GRATEFUL FOR ...

♡

♡

♡

♡

♡

♡

♡

♡

♡

INTENTION FOR THE DAY

MY DAILY AFFIRMATIONS

-
-
-
-
-

Friday

I AM MANIFESTING ...

....

....

....

....

HOW DO I WANT TO FEEL TODAY?

....

....

TODAY I AM GRATEFUL FOR ...

♡ ....

♡ ....

♡ ....

♡ ....

♡ ....

♡ ....

♡ ....

♡ ....

♡ ....

INTENTION FOR THE DAY

MY DAILY AFFIRMATIONS

● ....

● ....

● ....

● ....

● ....

Saturday

DATE: _____

I AM MANIFESTING ...

_____

_____

_____

HOW DO I WANT TO FEEL TODAY?

_____

_____

INTENTION FOR THE DAY

TODAY I AM GRATEFUL FOR ...

♡ _____

♡ _____

♡ _____

♡ _____

♡ _____

♡ _____

♡ _____

♡ _____

♡ _____

MY DAILY AFFIRMATIONS

● _____

● _____

● _____

● _____

● _____

Sunday

I AM MANIFESTING ...

....

....

....

HOW DO I WANT TO FEEL TODAY?

....

....

TODAY I AM GRATEFUL FOR ...

♡

♡

♡

♡

♡

♡

♡

♡

♡

INTENTION FOR THE DAY

MY DAILY AFFIRMATIONS

● ....

● ....

● ....

● ....

● ....

WEEK OF

(J) (F) (M) (A) (M) (J)
(J) (A) (S) (O) (N) (D)

INTENTION FOR THE WEEK

TOP 3 PRIORITIES

#**1**

#**2**

#**3**

THIS WEEK'S GOAL

INTENTIONAL ACTION STEPS

○
○
○
○
○
○
○
○
○

TRACKER	MO	TU	WE	TH	FR	SA	SU
Daily Gratitude	○	○	○	○	○	○	○
Affirmations	○	○	○	○	○	○	○
Visualization	○	○	○	○	○	○	○
Meditation	○	○	○	○	○	○	○
	○	○	○	○	○	○	○
	○	○	○	○	○	○	○
	○	○	○	○	○	○	○
	○	○	○	○	○	○	○

Monday

DATE: ....

I AM MANIFESTING ...

....

....

....

....

HOW DO I WANT TO FEEL TODAY?

....

....

....

TODAY I AM GRATEFUL FOR ...

♡ ....

♡ ....

♡ ....

♡ ....

♡ ....

♡ ....

♡ ....

♡ ....

♡ ....

INTENTION FOR THE DAY

MY DAILY AFFIRMATIONS

● ....

● ....

● ....

● ....

● ....

Tuesday

DATE: _____

I AM MANIFESTING ...

_____

_____

_____

_____

HOW DO I WANT TO FEEL TODAY?

_____

_____

_____

TODAY I AM GRATEFUL FOR ...

♡ _____

♡ _____

♡ _____

♡ _____

♡ _____

♡ _____

♡ _____

♡ _____

♡ _____

INTENTION FOR THE DAY

MY DAILY AFFIRMATIONS

● _____

● _____

● _____

● _____

● _____

Wednesday

I AM MANIFESTING ...

....

....

....

....

HOW DO I WANT TO FEEL TODAY?

....

....

....

TODAY I AM GRATEFUL FOR ...

♡ ....

♡ ....

♡ ....

♡ ....

♡ ....

♡ ....

♡ ....

♡ ....

♡ ....

INTENTION FOR THE DAY

MY DAILY AFFIRMATIONS

● ....

● ....

● ....

● ....

● ....

Thursday

DATE: _____

I AM MANIFESTING ...

_____

. . . .

. . . .

. . . .

HOW DO I WANT TO FEEL TODAY?

. . . .

. . . .

. . . .

TODAY I AM GRATEFUL FOR ...

♡

♡

♡

♡

♡

♡

♡

♡

♡

INTENTION FOR THE DAY

MY DAILY AFFIRMATIONS

● . . . .

● . . . .

● . . . .

● . . . .

● . . . .

Friday

I AM MANIFESTING ...

....

....

....

....

HOW DO I WANT TO FEEL TODAY?

....

....

....

INTENTION FOR THE DAY

TODAY I AM GRATEFUL FOR ...

♡ ....

♡ ....

♡ ....

♡ ....

♡ ....

♡ ....

♡ ....

♡ ....

♡ ....

MY DAILY AFFIRMATIONS

● ....

● ....

● ....

● ....

● ....

Saturday

DATE: ....

I AM MANIFESTING ...

....

....

....

....

HOW DO I WANT TO FEEL TODAY?

....

....

....

TODAY I AM GRATEFUL FOR ...

♡ ....

♡ ....

♡ ....

♡ ....

♡ ....

♡ ....

♡ ....

♡ ....

♡ ....

INTENTION FOR THE DAY

MY DAILY AFFIRMATIONS

● ....

● ....

● ....

● ....

● ....

Sunday

I AM MANIFESTING ...

....

....

....

....

HOW DO I WANT TO FEEL TODAY?

....

....

....

TODAY I AM GRATEFUL FOR ...

♡ ....

♡ ....

♡ ....

♡ ....

♡ ....

♡ ....

♡ ....

♡ ....

♡ ....

INTENTION FOR THE DAY

MY DAILY AFFIRMATIONS

● ....

● ....

● ....

● ....

● ....

WEEK OF

(J) (F) (M) (A) (M) (J)
(J) (A) (S) (O) (N) (D)

INTENTION FOR THE WEEK

TOP 3 PRIORITIES

#1 ....
#2 ....
#3 ....

INTENTIONAL ACTION STEPS

○ ....
○ ....
○ ....
○ ....
○ ....
○ ....
○ ....
○ ....
○ ....

THIS WEEK'S GOAL

TRACKER	MO	TU	WE	TH	FR	SA	SU
Daily Gratitude	○	○	○	○	○	○	○
Affirmations	○	○	○	○	○	○	○
Visualization	○	○	○	○	○	○	○
Meditation	○	○	○	○	○	○	○
	○	○	○	○	○	○	○
	○	○	○	○	○	○	○
	○	○	○	○	○	○	○
	○	○	○	○	○	○	○

Monday

I AM MANIFESTING ...

....

....

....

....

HOW DO I WANT TO FEEL TODAY?

....

....

....

TODAY I AM GRATEFUL FOR ...

♡ ....

♡ ....

♡ ....

♡ ....

♡ ....

♡ ....

♡ ....

♡ ....

♡ ....

INTENTION FOR THE DAY

MY DAILY AFFIRMATIONS

● ....

● ....

● ....

● ....

● ....

Tuesday

DATE:

I AM MANIFESTING ...

HOW DO I WANT TO FEEL TODAY?

TODAY I AM GRATEFUL FOR ...

♡

♡

♡

♡

INTENTION FOR THE DAY

♡

♡

♡

♡

MY DAILY AFFIRMATIONS

- ●
- ●
- ●
- ●
- ●

Wednesday

DATE:

I AM MANIFESTING ...

HOW DO I WANT TO FEEL TODAY?

TODAY I AM GRATEFUL FOR ...

♡

♡

♡

♡

♡

♡

♡

♡

♡

INTENTION FOR THE DAY

MY DAILY AFFIRMATIONS

●

●

●

●

●

Thursday

DATE: ....

I AM MANIFESTING ...

....

....

....

....

HOW DO I WANT TO FEEL TODAY?

....

....

....

TODAY I AM GRATEFUL FOR ...

♡ ....

♡ ....

♡ ....

♡ ....

♡ ....

♡ ....

♡ ....

♡ ....

♡ ....

INTENTION FOR THE DAY

MY DAILY AFFIRMATIONS

● ....

● ....

● ....

● ....

● ....

Friday

I AM MANIFESTING ...

....

....

....

....

HOW DO I WANT TO FEEL TODAY?

....

....

....

INTENTION FOR THE DAY

TODAY I AM GRATEFUL FOR ...

♡

♡

♡

♡

♡

♡

♡

♡

♡

MY DAILY AFFIRMATIONS

● ....

● ....

● ....

● ....

● ....

Saturday

DATE: _____

I AM MANIFESTING ...

_____

_____

_____

_____

HOW DO I WANT TO FEEL TODAY?

_____

_____

_____

TODAY I AM GRATEFUL FOR ...

♡ _____

♡ _____

♡ _____

♡ _____

♡ _____

♡ _____

♡ _____

♡ _____

♡ _____

INTENTION FOR THE DAY

MY DAILY AFFIRMATIONS

● _____

● _____

● _____

● _____

● _____

Sunday

I AM MANIFESTING ...

....

....

....

....

HOW DO I WANT TO FEEL TODAY?

....

....

....

TODAY I AM GRATEFUL FOR ...

♡ ....

♡ ....

♡ ....

♡ ....

♡ ....

♡ ....

♡ ....

♡ ....

♡ ....

INTENTION FOR THE DAY

MY DAILY AFFIRMATIONS

● ....

● ....

● ....

● ....

● ....

WEEK OF

(J) (F) (M) (A) (M) (J)
(J) (A) (S) (O) (N) (D)

INTENTION FOR THE WEEK

TOP 3 PRIORITIES

#1

#2

#3

THIS WEEK'S GOAL

INTENTIONAL ACTION STEPS

○
○
○
○
○
○
○
○
○

TRACKER	MO	TU	WE	TH	FR	SA	SU
Daily Gratitude	○	○	○	○	○	○	○
Affirmations	○	○	○	○	○	○	○
Visualization	○	○	○	○	○	○	○
Meditation	○	○	○	○	○	○	○
	○	○	○	○	○	○	○
	○	○	○	○	○	○	○
	○	○	○	○	○	○	○
	○	○	○	○	○	○	○

Monday

I AM MANIFESTING ...

....

....

....

....

HOW DO I WANT TO FEEL TODAY?

....

....

....

TODAY I AM GRATEFUL FOR ...

♡ ....

♡ ....

♡ ....

♡ ....

♡ ....

♡ ....

♡ ....

♡ ....

♡ ....

INTENTION FOR THE DAY

MY DAILY AFFIRMATIONS

● ....

● ....

● ....

● ....

● ....

Tuesday

DATE: ....

I AM MANIFESTING ...

....

....

....

....

HOW DO I WANT TO FEEL TODAY?

....

....

....

TODAY I AM GRATEFUL FOR ...

♡ ....

♡ ....

♡ ....

♡ ....

♡ ....

♡ ....

♡ ....

♡ ....

♡ ....

INTENTION FOR THE DAY

MY DAILY AFFIRMATIONS

● ....

● ....

● ....

● ....

● ....

Wednesday

DATE: ....

I AM MANIFESTING ...

....

....

....

....

HOW DO I WANT TO FEEL TODAY?

....

....

....

TODAY I AM GRATEFUL FOR ...

♡ ....

♡ ....

♡ ....

♡ ....

♡ ....

♡ ....

♡ ....

♡ ....

♡ ....

INTENTION FOR THE DAY

MY DAILY AFFIRMATIONS

● ....

● ....

● ....

● ....

● ....

Thursday

DATE: ....

I AM MANIFESTING ...

....

....

....

....

HOW DO I WANT TO FEEL TODAY?

....

....

....

TODAY I AM GRATEFUL FOR ...

♡ ....

♡ ....

♡ ....

♡ ....

♡ ....

♡ ....

♡ ....

♡ ....

♡ ....

INTENTION FOR THE DAY

MY DAILY AFFIRMATIONS

● ....

● ....

● ....

● ....

● ....

Friday

DATE: ....

I AM MANIFESTING ...

....

....

....

....

HOW DO I WANT TO FEEL TODAY?

....

....

....

TODAY I AM GRATEFUL FOR ...

♡ ....

♡ ....

♡ ....

♡ ....

♡ ....

♡ ....

♡ ....

♡ ....

♡ ....

INTENTION FOR THE DAY

MY DAILY AFFIRMATIONS

● ....

● ....

● ....

● ....

● ....

Saturday

DATE: _____

I AM MANIFESTING ...

_____

....

....

....

HOW DO I WANT TO FEEL TODAY?

....

....

....

INTENTION FOR THE DAY

TODAY I AM GRATEFUL FOR ...

♡

♡

♡

♡

♡

♡

♡

♡

♡

MY DAILY AFFIRMATIONS

● _____

● _____

● _____

● _____

● _____

Sunday

I AM MANIFESTING ...

....

....

....

HOW DO I WANT TO FEEL TODAY?

....

....

TODAY I AM GRATEFUL FOR ...

♡

♡

♡

♡

♡

♡

♡

♡

♡

INTENTION FOR THE DAY

MY DAILY AFFIRMATIONS

● ....

● ....

● ....

● ....

● ....

WEEK OF

(J) (F) (M) (A) (M) (J)
(J) (A) (S) (O) (N) (D)

INTENTION FOR THE WEEK

TOP 3 PRIORITIES

#**1**

#**2**

#**3**

INTENTIONAL ACTION STEPS

◯
◯
◯
◯
◯
◯
◯
◯
◯

THIS WEEK'S GOAL

TRACKER	MO	TU	WE	TH	FR	SA	SU
Daily Gratitude	◯	◯	◯	◯	◯	◯	◯
Affirmations	◯	◯	◯	◯	◯	◯	◯
Visualization	◯	◯	◯	◯	◯	◯	◯
Meditation	◯	◯	◯	◯	◯	◯	◯
	◯	◯	◯	◯	◯	◯	◯
	◯	◯	◯	◯	◯	◯	◯
	◯	◯	◯	◯	◯	◯	◯
	◯	◯	◯	◯	◯	◯	◯

Monday

I AM MANIFESTING ...

....

....

....

....

HOW DO I WANT TO FEEL TODAY?

....

....

....

TODAY I AM GRATEFUL FOR ...

♡ ....

♡ ....

♡ ....

♡ ....

♡ ....

♡ ....

♡ ....

♡ ....

♡ ....

INTENTION FOR THE DAY

MY DAILY AFFIRMATIONS

● ....

● ....

● ....

● ....

● ....

Tuesday

DATE: _____

I AM MANIFESTING ...

_____

_____

_____

_____

HOW DO I WANT TO FEEL TODAY?

_____

_____

_____

TODAY I AM GRATEFUL FOR ...

♡ _____

♡ _____

♡ _____

♡ _____

♡ _____

♡ _____

♡ _____

♡ _____

♡ _____

INTENTION FOR THE DAY

MY DAILY AFFIRMATIONS

● _____

● _____

● _____

● _____

● _____

Wednesday

I AM MANIFESTING ...

....

....

....

....

....

HOW DO I WANT TO FEEL TODAY?	TODAY I AM GRATEFUL FOR ...

HOW DO I WANT TO FEEL TODAY?

....

....

....

INTENTION FOR THE DAY

TODAY I AM GRATEFUL FOR ...

♡ ....

♡ ....

♡ ....

♡ ....

♡ ....

♡ ....

♡ ....

♡ ....

♡ ....

MY DAILY AFFIRMATIONS

● ....

● ....

● ....

● ....

● ....

Thursday

DATE: ....

I AM MANIFESTING ...

....

....

....

....

HOW DO I WANT TO FEEL TODAY?

....

....

....

INTENTION FOR THE DAY

TODAY I AM GRATEFUL FOR ...

♡

♡

♡

♡

♡

♡

♡

♡

♡

MY DAILY AFFIRMATIONS

● ....

● ....

● ....

● ....

● ....

Friday

DATE:

I AM MANIFESTING ...

HOW DO I WANT TO FEEL TODAY?

TODAY I AM GRATEFUL FOR ...

♡
♡
♡
♡
♡
♡
♡
♡
♡

INTENTION FOR THE DAY

MY DAILY AFFIRMATIONS

Saturday

I AM MANIFESTING ...

HOW DO I WANT TO FEEL TODAY?

TODAY I AM GRATEFUL FOR ...

♡

♡

♡

♡

♡

♡

♡

♡

♡

INTENTION FOR THE DAY

MY DAILY AFFIRMATIONS

-
-
-
-
-

Sunday

DATE:

I AM MANIFESTING ...

HOW DO I WANT TO FEEL TODAY?

TODAY I AM GRATEFUL FOR ...

♡

♡

♡

♡

INTENTION FOR THE DAY

♡

♡

♡

♡

♡

MY DAILY AFFIRMATIONS

Final Thoughts

Affirmations

Affirmations are very powerful. By saying, hearing or writing a powerful affirmation, you are programming your subconscious mind to be aligned with your desires.

In this way, it is possible to reprogram your brain and even overwrite deeply rooted limiting beliefs with new, empowering ones. And a new belief system is equal to a new reality.

Because your beliefs are like filters for your reality. What you think, you become.

The best way to get started with affirmations is to choose an area of your life you want to focus on. Below is a list of affirmations that might resonate with you. You can pick affirmations from this list and add them to your daily scripting pages.

Money

Money comes to me easily and effortlessly.

I constantly attract opportunities that create more money.

I am worthy of making more money.

I am open and receptive to all the wealth life offers me.

My actions create constant prosperity.

Money and spirituality can co-exist in harmony.

Love & Relationships

I am full of positive loving energy.

I welcome love and romance into my life.

I am in a loving and supportive relationship.

I deserve love and I get it in abundance.

I am loved, loving and lovable.

I am blessed with an incredible family and wonderful friends.

I give out love and it is returned to me multiplied manyfold.

Self

I forgive myself and set myself free.

I believe I can be all that I want to be.

I am in the process of becoming the best version of myself.

I have the freedom & power to create the life I desire.

I choose to be kind to myself and love myself unconditionally.

My possibilities are endless.

I am worthy of my dreams.

Health

I deserve to be healthy and feel good.

I am full of energy and vitality and my mind is calm and peaceful.

Every day I am getting healthier and stronger.

our my body by trusting the signals that it sends me.

anifest perfect health by making smart choices.

Printed in Great Britain
by Amazon

86462794R00066